MANAGEMENT
Destiny to Success

GUY BROWN

Management
Destiny to Success
All Rights Reserved.
Copyright © 2019 Guy Brown
v2.0

The opinions expressed in this manuscript are solely the opinions of the author and do not represent the opinions or thoughts of the publisher. The author has represented and warranted full ownership and/or legal right to publish all the materials in this book.

This book may not be reproduced, transmitted, or stored in whole or in part by any means, including graphic, electronic, or mechanical without the express written consent of the publisher except in the case of brief quotations embodied in critical articles and reviews.

Outskirts Press, Inc.
http://www.outskirtspress.com

ISBN: 978-1-9772-1544-4

Cover Photo © 2019 www.gettyimages.com. All rights reserved - used with permission.

Outskirts Press and the "OP" logo are trademarks belonging to Outskirts Press, Inc.

PRINTED IN THE UNITED STATES OF AMERICA

TABLE OF CONTENTS

Introduction	1
Stage 1	2
Stage 2	3
Stage 3	4
Stage 4	5
Stage 5	6
IMAGE	7
Points of Character	8
Motivation	10
Personal Questions	11
Productive Management	13
Complete Leadership	14
Recipe	16
Managing in a Circle	17
Gears of Thought	18

INTRODUCTION

The year was 1985, and a person with no direction was thrust into a supervisor's role with no experience or guidance. **I was that person.** I soon realized the qualities of a supervisor or manager are not taught, but developed. Through years of building characteristics which defined my success, I not only showed others how successful I could be , but I showed many how I could develop others to be successful.

Productive Management is not an art or science, but a daily display of decision making that produces results and accomplishments. I created this tool to assist others in building their foundation to become the best. I have been complimented many times in my career. I have had awards created to recognize my contributions, and I have been admired for my hard work and dedication. But my most rewarding moment was being thanked for helping a first time manager understand what it means to be a Productive Manager.

I hope the following will assist you in becoming the manager or supervisor that you strive to be. Your success with the help of this tool will be determined by how passionate you are to become better. Management is a great responsibility and through that position you are the gauge of other's success.

GLBJ

STAGE 1

The **Position Manager** is simply ecstatic to poses the title "Manager". He still has all the characteristics of an entry level manager, yet now he has a title. He is excited everyday to come to work so his supervisor and his peers can see him carry the title of manager. This manager continues to work hard and is willing to do whatever it takes to be viewed as a manager.

He is aware of his deficiencies but goes through his day hoping he will see some action that will assist him in resolving any managerial challenge he may encounter.

He truly has the desire to grow as a manager but does not have the maturity or self confidence to seek out avenues of improvement and self growth. This manager is normally in a position to maintain front line productivity.

"You can build upon this Manager"

STAGE 2

The **Money Made Manager** is driven solely by his salary. In this position his income allows him to have discretionary money on a consistent basis. Others view him as a personable person that never lives pay check to pay check.

He performs his job duties well enough to show positive results and maintain productivity, yet his every action is to confirm hours worked.

This manager will perform as directed and ensure he is viewed as a manager who is worthy of his salary.

"You can build with this Manager"

STAGE 3

The **Power Manager** bases his performance on instilling in others that his position has power over them. He tends to use intimidation in his communication and actions. This manager is occasionally boisterous when speaking to subordinates. He lacks the ability to think as a controlled manager so he mask areas of uncertainty behind his display of power within his position.

Although this manager may not always portray consistent professionalism, he will be aggressive in achieving results. When there is a strong team assembled he, more likely than not, will be the manager to aggressively communicate the plan, course, and actions to achieve results.

"You can build around this Manager"

STAGE 4

The **Promotable Manager** is confident in his ability to perform to an exceptional level. He understands his job duties and is viewed to be a top performer on a consistent basis. This manager can independently execute under adverse conditions and provide effective solutions. Most peers request of him advice and suggestions to improve their productivity.

Under all circumstances this manager incorporates 3 characteristics into his daily operations: Sound Leadership, Adaptability, and a Sense of Urgency.

He aspires to be the best in his class of management. He produces results and normally has managers under his supervision that believe strongly in his ability. He can flawlessly manage operations within his position and produce above average top line results.

"You can build beside this Manager"

STAGE 5

The **Business Owner Manager** is the complete manager. He has knowledge of every aspect of the business and understands how to perform, coach, and develop areas to produce results. He illuminates confidence and his presence demands respect. This manager has the ability to discern all challenges and implement a solution which produces results.

This manager uses his knowledge and experience to build a business model that can prosper in any environment. He creates procedures and standards that give sound direction to any business. This manager carries himself in a professional manner thinks business first.

The performance of this manager is an asset. He has extensive knowledge, an aggressive attitude to succeed, and the drive to capitalize on every opportunity. Because he is a professional , he knows how to adapt to situations and put himself in a position to be viewed as a team player. This manager can manage within any environment while producing outstanding results . **He is a winner.**

" This manager <u>WILL</u> build your business"

IMAGE

I   INVOLVED   (An employee can only establish a positive image of you as a manager if he/she views you as being actively involved in day-to-day operations)

M   MANAGABLE   (To maintain a high level of open communication between you and your immediate supervisor, you must give the impression you are open to the knowledge and teaching of others)

A   AGGRESSIVE   (Results can only be achieved if you aggressively focus yourself and others on the end result)

G   GOAL-ORIENTED   (Every task has a goal of achievement, and in order to achieve success of a task, you must first display the targeted goal)

E   ESTABLISHED   (In your day-to-day operations, allow your strong and successful management qualities to be visible to both those who work for you as well as above you)

POINTS OF CHARACTER

Professionalism

- Before you do or say something, **Think :** can this offend, upset, or degrade someone else?
- Your comments , actions, and directives should be in a manner that you would like them to be directed towards you.
- Don't allow your personal feelings to be a factor in your actions and reactions.
- Treat all positions the same, regardless of your personal feelings and with **RESPECT.**

Adaptability

- Be able to provide structure at the immediate point of a hectic time.
- Show you know how to give directions to everyone working under your supervision when it's not hectic or there are times of non-productivity.
- Be able to analyze numerous situations, provide good service , and provide direction at your most stressful time.

Maturity

- Think as a professional, carry yourself as a professional, and react as a professional.
- Never put yourself in a position to be viewed as a "kid". Never act in a manner which those working with you can view you as "childish"

MOTIVATION

Being In the position you are, you are looked upon for guidance and support. It is your responsibility to reassure all employees that you are interested in his/her well-being and success. The same attention and assistance given to your most promotable employee should be extended to a stagnated employee as well.

A Good Manager or Supervisor has ...

- the ability to teach and develop
- the ability to support all employees
- the ability to correct and resolve
- the ability to recognize and reward
- the ability to keep everyone informed
- the ability to consult and delegate

Characteristics of a Good Manager or Supervisor...

- Fair
- Problem Solver
- Possess High Standards
- Tactful and Diplomatic
- Approachable
- Considerate
- Consistent

PERSONAL QUESTIONS

For every complaint of an **inexperienced manager**, there are personal questions which he/she should ask themselves.

1. **Complaint:** "These guys don't do anything but sit around and complain"

Personal Question: How often do I allow my employees to have idle time that interrupts productivity?

2. **Complaint:** "I am tired of telling this guy to straighten up his act"

Personal Question: How consistent have I been on enforcing policy and procedure violations?

3. **Complaint :** "It doesn't matter how many times I talk to these guys, I don't see changes"

Personal Questions: Out of all my counseling sessions, how many times have I demand a particular goal be obtained, and have I assisted this employee in obtaining that goal?

4. **Complaint :** "They are so behind on their work load"

Personal Question: Do I perform enough follow-ups and evaluations of individual performances?

5. Complaint : "I don't have time to baby-sit these guys"

Personal Question: Do I create an atmosphere conducive to the conduct of business in a mature and professional manner?

6. Complaint : "This person's attitude is affecting everyone else"

Personal Question: Do I attack and resolve a negative attitude that could affect others?

7. Complaint : "I would rather take a transfer than to keep putting up with this mess"

Personal Question: Have I made an attempt to resolve every problem and am convinced there is no possible solution?

8. Complaint : "I want everyone to get along in this operation"

Personal Question: Am I asking the impossible? Or should I try to maintain a pleasant work environment conducive to productivity?

9. Complaint: "I don't want a lot of race issues to continue coming up in this operation"

Personal Question: Do I allow employee's personal feelings and beliefs to interfere with job performance?

PRODUCTIVE MANAGEMENT

There are **Three** common characteristics shared by productive managers who are successful in **Sales** and **Customer Satisfaction:**

Focused-Leadership

Adaptability

Sense of Urgency

COMPLETE LEADERSHIP

Foundation of the Perfect Manager

* **Complete Knowledge of Position**
* **High Performance Standards**
* **Many styles of Training**
* **Able to Motivate and Reward**
* **Result Oriented**
* **Resolve complaints and issue compliments**
* **Focus on Morale**

1. Aware of position standards

    As part of the controlling element of your operation, you should be aware of the standards of your job duties. This will assist you in making decisions, suggestions, and corrections within your operation. You are not performing to standards if your immediate supervisor does not have the same perception of you as he/she does of themselves.

2. Goal and Task Setting

   Because you are part of leadership in your operation you are expected to implement goals and tasks that enable you to recognize and resolve all problems , hazards, and distractions to the safety , appearance , and productivity of the overall operation.

3. Increase Organization and Productivity

   Organization and cleanliness in all areas of the operations is a must at all times. The more an operation is unorganized the greater chance a problem is being overshadowed . Under these circumstances , your operation will never reach it's full potential of profitability.

RECIPE

- A recipe for : **Success**

    1 ½ pounds of **Focus**

    1 pinch of **Determination**

    2 tablespoons of **Respect**

    4 cups of **Adaptability**

    2 gallons of **Consistency**

    1 package of **Self-Confidence**

    3 wheel barrels of **Effective Management**

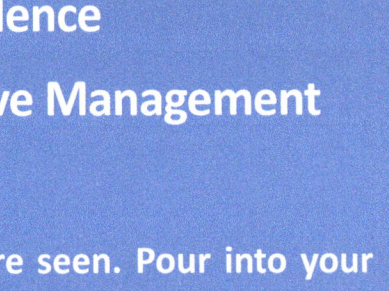

Mix well until RESULTS are seen. Pour into your daily operations. Insert into a PRODUCTIVE environment until done.

Remove, and reap the REWARDS

MANAGING IN A CIRCLE

Little or No Respect
Little or No Self-Discipline
Little or No Professionalism

There are numerous qualities of an unsuccessful manager. Typically , this manager experiences the same results in whatever task he/she accepts: **Failure**

There are normally 3 components of an unsuccessful manager: 1. Little or No Respect 2. Little or No Self-Discipline 3. Little or No Professionalism

A manager that manages in the model of a CIRCLE will never achieve their reward because there is no clear path to the point of success.

GEARS OF THOUGHT

A decision made on emotions lack foresight

Self-Discipline = the ability to consistently perform with tact, respect, and professionalism without the need of it being an addressed action

A good manager is a manager who has evaluated and replaced all characteristics which made him/her a bad manager

Management is viewed by its character and judged by its actions

Business Insanity – Doing things the same way over and over, expecting different results

www.ingramcontent.com/pod-product-compliance
Lightning Source LLC
Chambersburg PA
CBHW040519220526
45473CB00012B/2914